"Nathan Magnuson is a breath of fresh air in the smoke-filled back rooms of leadership theory. His voice is pragmatic, pointed, and passionate. Leaders need someone who is ahead of them on the journey to shout back both warnings and the way forward. Thanks, Nathan, for investing your leadership energy to serve others... not surprising you would - that's what great leaders do!"

Mark Miller
International Bestselling Author
Vice President, High Performance Leadership
Chick-fil-A, Inc.

"As someone who has served thousands of leaders over the years, I've learned that book smarts can only take you so far down the road of effective leadership. It's people smarts that allow great leaders to gain the trust and confidence of the ones they serve. Ignite Your Leadership Expertise shows how to grow them both in ways other people find helpful and meaningful. Great work, Nathan!"

Bob Tiede
Author of *Great Leaders ASK Questions*
Blogger at LeadingWithQuestions.com

IGNITE YOUR LEADERSHIP EXPERTISE

Become the Trusted
Advisor Others Seek

Nathan Magnuson

Ordering Information
Special discounts are available on quantity purchases by corporations, associations and others. For details, please use the contact address listed above.

Cover & book design: John W. Nichols

Independently Published
ISBN: 9781723841576

First Edition: October 2018

For Dr. Jeff Myers.
It was in your leadership class that I first realized all of this could be possible for me.
Thank you.

TABLE OF CONTENTS

INTRODUCTION

What does it really mean to be an expert — and a leadership expert at that?

Over the years as a leadership consultant for several Fortune 500 companies, I've witnessed countless colleagues, clients and friends suddenly catch the "leadership bug." Young professionals search for a positive example to follow. Veteran leaders want to discover the next secret to greater effectiveness. Maybe the most surprising shift I've noticed is established leaders who have focused mostly on their own technical proficiency for some time — often with significant success. All at once, something sparks a desire to take their leadership influence to the next level. They aren't satisfied making a functional contribution. They want to make a leadership contribution as well.

Here's what I can tell you: you don't need to be a member of the C-suite to be a leadership expert. You certainly don't need to be part of HR. I believe you can be an expert on leadership from right where you are, beginning right now. In fact, I know you can — if you'll use the tips in this book. Inside, you'll learn how to:

- Become a trusted leadership advisor that others in your organization and community begin to seek out and confide in.
- Confidently identify and share the leadership expertise you already possess for immediate impact with others.
- Grow your expertise further in both the short-term and long-term.
- Engage in active listening and ask powerful questions that drive deep connection with all types of leaders.
- Coach others to achieve clear outcomes without having a personal agenda.
- And much more...

Let's talk for a minute about how to use this book. My favorite part is that it's concise — only about 10,000 words, so you can implement the material quickly. It's divided into ten short topics. You'll get the most out of it by only reading one or two at a time. Each topic has a few questions to reflect on. The best approach is to enlist a buddy, small group or work team to read along with you. (If you work through this book with a group, drop me a note at nathan@nathanmagnuson.com and let me know how it goes.)

The world is crying out for positive leadership examples to follow. On a very individual level, people everywhere are looking for a leader who can spark their confidence, competence and *meaningful* performance outcomes. But they may never get there without your help. Will you give it to them?

Are you ready to be ignited? If so, let's get started!

PS — As a thank you for taking this journey with me, I'd like to share my white paper *Nine Ways to Be the Boss Everyone Wants to Work For.* You'll receive more information about this powerful resource at the end of the book.

BECOMING A TRUSTED LEADERSHIP ADVISOR

Has anyone ever asked you how to become a better leader? I remember the first time I was asked. It wasn't by a buddy, it was my dentist who had just bought out her practice and was trying to make it as a business owner as well. We'd been talking through some of her challenges together. I think I was 21 or 22 at the time. All of a sudden she put me on the spot and everything I thought I knew about leadership started to jumble together.

What does it *really* mean to be a leader, I wondered.

Since then, I've come to realize that most people don't start asking for help with leadership until they face a leadership challenge. Think about it — you don't call your auto mechanic to tell him your car has been running well lately. You probably don't call your counselor to share how well your relationships are going (although I'm sure he or she would love to hear it!). You seek them out when you're stuck — literally or figuratively! It's usually the same with leadership.

So what can you do when people ask for your leadership input? Here are three approaches I take:

1. Make leadership seem easier

Leadership isn't easy, mostly because life isn't easy. But poor leadership makes everything significantly more difficult. Poor leadership produces inferior outcomes and bruised followers. As Truett Cathy pointed out, "It really is easier to succeed than to fail, because when you fail you have to start all over again from a lesser position."[1]

There is no easy button for leadership. But when you can show people how making a difficult leadership decision now will create a better and less stressful future, you'll have their attention.

2. Make leadership seem less complicated

One of the realities of success is that it breeds complication. The more money you earn, the more complicated your taxes become. As your family grows, the more complicated your schedule becomes. Leadership is the same in that complication can be a side effect of success. What is different is that it's all-encompassing. As John Maxwell noted, "*Everything* rises and falls on leadership."

That said, you can make leadership seem less complicated for others by helping them identify the source of their leadership challenges.

When I take my car to the mechanic, I tell him what I'm experiencing and then he helps me diagnose the root issue. He doesn't keep me there until I understand everything about how my car works. (Thank God, because I'd be there forever!) Usually most of my car is working the way it should. You don't need a PhD in leadership to enjoy success or competently advise others. Simply help them distinguish between what is working well and the source of their problem. That will make leadership challenges much less complicated and easier to address.

3. Make leadership seem more fun

If you've caught the "leadership bug," one of the first things you may notice is that not everyone gets as excited about it as you are. But everyone wants to enjoy success in their work and life. Leadership undoubtedly plays a role.

You can help leadership seem more fun by helping people win on their terms. Zig Ziglar was famous for declaring, "You can have anything in life you want if you will just help enough other people get what they want."[2] When you can help others understand how effective leadership will help them succeed at the things that matter most to them, leadership becomes exciting! In fact, I would argue that if you're not having fun, you're doing it wrong! Do this, and you may be surprised when your not-so-enthusiastic-about-leadership friends start seeking your input.

"You can have anything in life you want if you will just help enough other people get what they want."

— Zig Ziglar

Questions for Reflection

- If someone asks you what it means to be a leader, how will you respond?
- What are some of the biggest leadership challenges the leaders around you face?
- What do the leaders around you want (e.g. make more money, save time, reduce stress, build a stronger team, etc.)? How can you discuss leadership specifically in terms of their desired outcomes?

THE THREE LEADERSHIP QUESTIONS I ALWAYS ASK

How do you talk with other people about leadership? Unless I'm already a trusted leadership advisor, most people don't just come up and ask me to help them evaluate their personal and organizational leadership effectiveness. (And when they do, it's a little more organic than that!) It's true the more responsibilities people acquire, the more complicated their leadership situation gets. Executive leaders usually have access to budget, resources and personnel to address the leadership challenges they face. Everyday leaders often have to figure things out on their own. You may be able to help, but how do you get the conversation started?

One of the things I've come to learn over the years (sometimes the hard way) is that people are often sensitive about their leadership challenges. They won't want to talk about it if they sense you have an agenda (even if the agenda is just to be helpful). And most of the time, it doesn't matter how much or little you know. You have to be invited. Another thing I've learned is that, among other things, *leadership is a conversation.*

So instead of trying to solve folks' leadership challenges for them, start with taking an interest in them as a person and inviting them into a natural conversation without an agenda. Don't start with what you know, but with the other person's situation. Follow Stephen Covey's fifth habit advice, "seek first to understand, then to be understood."[3] This way, whether or not you're asked for your input, the other leader knows that you care.

To help with these conversations, I've included my three favorite leadership questions to ask, whether I'm speaking with a new client for the first time, a friend or a new acquaintance. Instead of inviting myself to solve their problems, these questions help me invite others to talk about themselves. Here they are.

What are you working on that you're really excited about?

This is a great opening question because it engages the other person's positive emotions. People like talking about the things that get them excited. It highlights what is really working for them. No matter how challenging things may be, if there is something to get excited about, then hope is alive and well.

What would you like to get to next when you're able?

This is a great follow-up question because it speaks to the other person's goals or foresight. Do they possess a clear path forward or are they struggling to fight fires? Is the future likely to be more exciting down the road or bring more complications?

What concerns are you experiencing right now?

This is a very mild and non-intrusive way to inquire about problems the other leader is facing. Perhaps a more direct version is to ask, "What is keeping you up at night?" Instead of putting the other person on the defensive by insinuating they may be the cause, this question simply inquires about a feeling they possess. Everyone has concerns. Once you've engaged positive emotions, it's much easier to inquire about any negative ones.

By the way, you may not even have to ask this question. If the future looks complicated, the other leader may volunteer as much and tell you why.

At the end of a short conversation based on these three questions, you'll have a good grasp on what's working, what the plan is and what the challenges are. This puts you in a great position to provide input, offer a possible solution or to simply ask how you can provide support.

_____

"People don't care how much you know until they know how much you care."

— Theodore Roosevelt

_____

Theodore Roosevelt is credited with observing that, "People don't care how much you know until they know how much you care." Will you join me in leadership conversations that are unmistakably others-centered?

Questions for Reflection

- What role does trust plays in a leadership conversation?
- Who can you engage in a leadership conversation using these three questions?

THE BEST LEADERSHIP EDUCATION YOU CAN GET FOR FREE

Just about all of us are Monday morning quarterbacks when it comes to leadership. Everyone has an opinion. But how informed are those opinions, especially if we've never been there before?

Here's the thing: if you wait until you receive a leadership role to get a leadership education, you may be waiting for a long time and you may not last long once you get there. We all need a leadership development plan that includes work experiences, formal training, networking and self-study. But don't overlook the easiest, cheapest and most accessible one of all: observation.

Here are eight observations to make of the leaders around you.

How They Make Decisions

You can tell a lot about the leaders around you by the decisions they make — or don't make. One of the biggest frustrations to senior management is middle management who won't make the tough decisions at their level. As an observer, you obviously won't have access to all the same information, but you can still learn a lot.

How They Communicate with Their Teams

Engagement studies reveal that the majority of organizations have a "communication problem" — especially in the consistency and cascading of high-priority messages. Good leaders over-communicate what is truly important. Take special note of what the leaders around you decline to communicate publicly.

How They Organize Their Time and Priorities

A leader's time is of great value. It's a finite resource that must accommodate a growing number of responsibilities. Observe the systems they use to stay on top of schedule. Pay special attention to what they say "no" to.

How They Respond to Crises and Criticism

When Robert Mueller was confirmed as Director of the FBI, it wasn't because of his special ability to respond to crises. He specialized in white-collar crime. But one week later the World Trade Center was hit and Mueller became a full-time crisis manager. The leaders around you may not have to manage a catastrophe, but pay attention to the way they handle disruptions to their plans — and the public response they receive.

How Engaged Their People Are

It shouldn't come as a surprise that employees prefer to work for strong leaders. It's not because it's easier — many times it's not. Followers will usually work harder and stay later for a leader they respect. "A" leaders attract "A" followers who are engaged in the work, with the organization and with each other.

How Many Leaders They Produce

Did you know that leaders actually grow on trees? The best leaders develop and produce more leaders who in turn produce more. This may be most clearly seen in professional football "coaching trees," where nearly every successful coach cut his teeth under a previous successful coach. Figure out which leaders in your leadership community have the best reputation for developing talent — and take note of their approach.

What Results They Get

Execution is the bottom line of leadership effectiveness. Without it, leaders lose their opportunity, regardless of the circumstances. Leadership is a tough business. Always take note of the results the leaders around you achieve — especially if there are significant challenges.

It's easy to win when all the momentum is on your side. It's hard when the odds are against you.

The Mistakes They Make

This one is perhaps the most obvious and insightful. Every mistake of someone else's you learn from, you potentially avoid making yourself.

You've probably realized by now that not all the examples around you are good ones. A failure by one leader could mean you receive a new assignment before you're ready for it. Regardless, don't wait to build your leadership competency. You'll be able to share your informed observations with others in the meantime. So start taking notes today.

Every mistake of someone else's you learn from, you potentially avoid making yourself.

Questions for Reflection

- What leadership lessons have you learned from observation over the years?
- Which quality leaders can you pay extra attention to?
- Is there a leader from your past you want to avoid emulating at all costs? What will you do differently?

- Which emerging leader might benefit from one of your observations?

IT DOESN'T MATTER HOW MUCH YOU CARE

When I first began studying leadership years ago, I'd find myself in conversations when someone would invariably share a leadership challenge with me. Sometimes, I'd even know how to solve it. I'd usually reference a book or an idea I had recently studied. Sometimes in my enthusiasm, I'd even go out and purchase the resource for them. Unfortunately, when I followed up a few weeks later to find out what had happened, they had rarely bothered to look at what I had provided them.

Several years later, I got a lead role on a consulting assignment to develop a plan to significantly improve an organization's corporate culture. In fact, I was told this was my chance to "really shape the project." I spent the next few months analyzing employee survey data, referencing strategic plans and carefully crafting a solution. Finally I got to present my plan to a senior client in a boardroom meeting and was thrilled when he accepted it. Now it was time to get to work. But much to my chagrin, a bigger problem soon emerged: no one wanted to take responsibility for seeing the plan through.

These experiences confirmed for me a simple but poignant lesson: you can't want something for other people more than they want it for themselves. It doesn't matter how much you care if they don't.

This seems to go against the nature of empathy and basic altruism. But as a leadership principle, it's proved to be true for me.

You can't want something more for other people than they want it for themselves.

So what do you do *when you do care?* Here is the approach I've learned to take:

Inquire About Priority

When you talk, coach or consult with others, hopefully they trust you enough to share their challenges with you. But just like our own thoughts or mindless complaints, at any given time their concerns can range from short-term or inconsequential to long-term, significant or overwhelming. Not every problem carries equal weight and requires an immediate solution — or even any solution at all. Instead of assuming a person is looking for answers, try to get a sense of the priority the challenge represents. There is a big difference between a level 1 "would be nice to fix" challenge and a level 5 "front page headline" challenge.

Understand Commitment

If I had to do the culture transformation project over again, I would have asked a simple question before I even got started: who from the client team will be the executive sponsor for this solution after the planning phase is finished? Not understanding local commitment was an oversight on my part. You can avoid that mistake by pressing the issue upfront. The perfect plan with no commitment provides no benefit. It's a complete waste of time and effort. Not only will commitment help you manage your expectations, it will help the other party decide if a solution is worth pursuing in the first place.

Ask the Ultimate Question

I mentioned above how I used to take the responsibility to try and solve the leadership challenges I encountered. I don't do this anymore. It was hard to resist at first, but I've learned a much better way. It comes in the form of what I call the ultimate leadership question:

How would you like me to support you?

This question almost works like magic. It leaves all the responsibility where it belongs: with the party who has a challenge. But it communicates that you are willing help. And it gives the other person a variety of choices to make: do they prefer to tackle this challenge on their own, would they like a helping hand or do they prefer to leave it be for another day?

Jack Welch said that if you don't like people, you should find another job because leadership is 70% people development.[4] If you're going to be a leader, you need to care about other people. But caring about them shouldn't supersede the principle of boundaries. To empower others to drive change, you must keep your initiative in check. If you find that you care more about their outcome than they do, you may be headed for trouble.

Questions for Reflection

- Have you ever tried to help a friend or colleague who wouldn't (or couldn't) move forward? What do you think was the issue?
- Have you ever been completely off-base about the priority level of a project at work? What do you wish you had done differently?
- What is your next immediate opportunity to ask the ultimate question, "How would you like me to support you?"

HOW TO BECOME A LEADERSHIP EXPERT, PART 1

At a social function recently I found myself in an engaging conversation with a psychologist and a fitness coach. We took turns sharing the interesting nuances of our professions. After my turn explaining the exciting ways I get to be involved in leadership as a consultant, coach and writer, one of my new friends commented that leadership goes hand-in-hand with both psychology and fitness. I asked what he meant. He clarified that commitment to developing a healthy body and a sound mind are some of the first traits necessary to lead oneself and others. "But," he added, "I'd feel awkward presenting myself as a leadership expert. Who am I to say I know what leadership is and that people should listen to me?"

It was such a great question. Who are the real leadership experts anyway? Are they the people who manage Fortune 500 companies, hold elected positions or write bestselling books? They certainly qualify, but are there others?

I'm convinced everyone can become not only a leader but an expert as well, because we all have the ability to influence and to learn and grow. That means you! And it can happen much sooner than you think. What a great loss it would be for anyone to sidestep their leadership potential because they felt unqualified. So let me share my rationale with you. You can become a leadership expert from right where you are, starting today.

You are most likely already a leadership expert to someone.

Each of us has a leadership community — people we influence and are influenced by; people we're responsible for and who are responsible for us. Some of our leadership communities are large and some are small. As we grow, our communities grow as well.

But regardless of the size of your leadership community or platform, it is almost certain that someone looks to you for influence. This means you are an "expert" to them. If you are a supervisor, your leadership expertise probably influences your subordinates more than any other person's. The same can be said if you are the parent of young children. If you operate a business, at some level you are an expert to your customers. If you write or blog, you influence your readers. If you interact with, instruct, or teach others, you are an expert to them. Friends who value your advice on anything at all (including leadership) consider you an expert enough to ask.

A title does not make a leader.

Just because people don't introduce you as a "leadership expert" doesn't mean you can't be one. John Maxwell says that *everything rises and falls on leadership*. That means no matter what title you hold or what profession you're in, you are also in the leadership business. Very few people are solely leadership specialists. Virtually all of the high profile leadership experts are considered as such because of knowledge, skill or experience in a certain industry or organization. So whether you are in psychology, fitness or anything else, succeeding in that field makes you a leader. Taking the opportunity to develop and share your knowledge and experience with others makes you an expert.

Leadership is a journey, not a destination.

If no one could become a leadership expert until they figured out everything there is to know about leadership, we simply wouldn't have any leadership experts around. There's always much more to learn! We're all works in progress, which means you'll never have it completely figured out. But that doesn't mean you can't be an expert on what you've learned so far — and your expertise will deepen as you grow. The insight you gain today can be someone else's breakthrough tomorrow — provided you share it with them.

You're never too unqualified to set a good example — and that includes setting a good leadership example.

If you don't remember any of the other points, remember this one. We are never too unqualified to set a good leadership example. Sometimes we do need certain titles or certifications to make specific leadership decisions. But at its pure foundation, leadership is about serving others — something anyone can do. Being a leadership expert is a volunteer opportunity. Many times it's not particularly glamorous, but it's one of the only ways to truly earn the opportunity to influence.

You're never too unqualified to set a good example.

Questions for Reflection

- Have you ever considered yourself to be a leadership expert? How does it feel? Exciting? Intimidating?
- Who do you have influence with now — especially with regard to leadership? Rapidly list as many people as you can think of.
- What is one way you can volunteer to set a better leadership example right where you are?

HOW TO BECOME A LEADERSHIP EXPERT, PART 2

In the last section I shared several reasons why you don't have to wait until later to be a leadership expert. You can begin right here, right now, no matter who you are. If you've bought that idea, then let me share several practical ways to use your leadership expertise to benefit others.

Engage others in leadership conversations and listen well.

You've already seen the three leadership questions I ask, whether I'm speaking with someone for the first time or with my close friends. They actually don't feel like "leadership" questions at all, but by the end of the conversation, I have a good understanding of the basic leadership situation they are dealing with. I know what's working and what's not. Leadership isn't always about sharing what you know with others. In fact, that's never the right place to start. The better you become at encouraging others to talk about themselves, listening to them and truly understanding their situation, it's uncanny how much you will grow as a leadership expert in their eyes.

Share what you've observed.

No matter how much or how little "real world" experience you have, you've observed leadership in action. You've seen things that have worked well and you've seen things that haven't worked at all. You've seen things that started out well but ended up poorly. *Always pay attention to the leadership mindsets, decision-making process and execution that happens around you.* Use those learning points to inform what you know about leadership, and then share them with others. Learning from the successes and failures of others is as free a leadership education as it gets.

———

Learning from the successes and failures of others is as free a leadership education as it gets.

———

Share the things you've learned through experience.

It's hard to learn how to lead people if you never do it yourself. Therefore, your own experiences in leading others can be the quickest and sharpest developmental points you get. For better or worse, you are always the expert on your own experience. It won't take long before you have a list of what works well and what doesn't work at all. Don't keep this to yourself! Help others go further faster by sharing what you've learned through experience. And incidentally, don't be afraid to share your mistakes — sometimes people relate to them much more than to your successes.

Share the ideas you've developed.

As a student of leadership, you're probably on the lookout for ways to lead more effectively. At the beginning, all you have are untested theories. Keep it up and eventually you may discover the "Higgs Boson" of leadership. (Hey, it's possible!) But regardless of your progress, don't keep from sharing your ideas with others who could use them, whether it's on a napkin at a restaurant or publishing a white paper. Even scientists have to start with a hypothesis in order to find the solutions they are looking for. (You'll need to get your own peer-reviews just like they do!) Even if your ideas aren't perfect, they are better than none and often a great place to start.

Share what other experts are saying.

Don't just develop your own ideas in isolation. Even the top leadership experts pull from what others have said about leadership. You can use the best of the incredible things you've found that others have shared. Another perk is that you benefit from the association. On top of that, if people don't like what you've passed along, they aren't disagreeing with you but with the person you referenced!

Subtly self-promote around areas of competence.

Depending on your personality, you could be the most competent leadership expert available but still have a hard time tooting your own leadership horn. (Disclaimer: I'm not sure these instruments actually exist.) Reconciling humility and leadership can be difficult for some of us. Learn to subtly self-promote around your areas of competence.[5] If you don't, not only will you miss a huge opportunity to share your influence, more importantly, those around you could end up following second-rate (or just plain terrible) leadership ideas instead of yours.

Serve.

I mentioned this in the last section as well, but it bears repeating. No matter your level of expertise, you are always qualified to set a good leadership example. Leadership is about putting others first and working toward the success of something bigger than yourself. There is no better way to earn the opportunity to influence others than to be willing to serve them.

Questions for Reflection

- What is one leadership lesson you've learned either from observation, experience or from another leadership expert?
- What is one of your own leadership theories?
- What is one area of strong competence? How can you humbly but assertively let others know they can and should count on you?

LISTEN YOUR WAY TO THE TOP

In recent years, we've seen a new emphasis placed on the art of listening. It can't be because listening is all of a sudden more important than it ever was before. Maybe the nature of work in the information age means the cost of misunderstanding is higher. Or perhaps the experts have been burned by poor listening one too many times and decided to produce more thought leadership on the topic.

At any rate, study after study demonstrates the importance of listening to communication, leadership and influence. We are apparently able to listen about three times faster than we can speak, but we also forget most of what we've heard. Listening has been identified as one of the top qualities employers seek. And the ability to listen well has been tied to the ability to lead. Leadership is impossible without communication and communication is impossible without listening.

Everyone wants to be hired, to lead well and to be understood. So how can we learn to listen more effectively? The first step is to distinguish between the various listening levels that exist. Here are five of the most common ones:

Leadership is impossible without communication and communication is impossible without listening.

Passive Listening

Passive listening occurs during nearly all of our waking moments. In passive listening, there is virtually no difference between communication we are receiving and the white noise we hear: traffic, background music, the sound of nature, etc. We tend to tune much of it out, especially if we are simultaneously speaking, concentrating or listening to something else. No meaningful communication can take place unless we give our full attention.

Selective Listening

Selective listening occurs when we tune in and out of our present circumstances or conversations. If you are in the car waiting for the traffic report on the radio, you may let your attention span wander until the report comes on. We often do this with people as well. Picture yourself at a dinner party. When the conversation holds no interest for you, you drift. But when it comes around to a topic where you have an opinion, you are much more likely to stay engaged. If you've ever tried to answer an email while a co-working was speaking with you, you probably subjected them to selective listening — and probably annoyed them as well.

Self-Focused Listening

Self-focused listening pays close attention for meaning, but only as it applies to one's self. If you have been in a work meeting where new upcoming changes were being announced for the first time, it's likely you were applying self-focused listening. You considered what the implications meant for you and whether they were positive or negative. If you see a news clip talking about changes to the tax codes, you will probably apply self-focused listening. The same thing happens in one-on-one conversations. Suppose you have a friend who recounts a recent heart attack. If your reaction is to consider whether you've had the same symptoms, you are engaged in self-focused listening.

Solution-Focused Listening

Solution-focused listening tends to come the most naturally to many of us, but can also be the most irritating of all the levels. It occurs whenever we simultaneously listen and begin to form our response to what is being communicated. We quickly translate the input (what we hear) into our own assessment (what we think) and then into new output (what we say). It requires a high level of engagement. Solution-focused listening is a must for situations when it's critical to think on your feet, such as public debates or managing an active crisis. But it can create significant misunderstanding or disillusionment in less urgent conversations. A solution-focused response is likely to be inaccurate (since it's based on limited understanding), inadequate (the listener hasn't had the same experience) or inappropriate (the communicator may not be seeking a solution at all). It can bring a premature end to the communication as well since the communicator can either take the solution or leave it.

Active Listening

Active listening is the highest level. It is listening for the sole purpose of understanding. Stephen Covey calls this "empathetic listening." Others refer to it as "intuitive listening." Active listeners have the self-discipline to resist forming a response and place all their focus on the communicator and the message. People who listen actively don't assume they have the complete picture once the other person stops talking. They repeat back or ask if their understanding is accurate. They may even ask follow-up questions in order to understand more fully. Once their understanding is confirmed, future communication and solution-finding are likely to be much more effective.

There you have it: five levels of listening. Some come naturally. Others require significant self-discipline. For leaders looking to grow their influence, active listening is a challenge worth accepting. It won't be easy at first;

you'll have to stick with it. But the change will be swift and noticeable — especially by the people you engage with.

Questions for Reflection

- Which listening level do you use most often?
- Which situations tempt you to use solution-focused listening?
- Who can you begin applying active listening with this week?

HOW TO ASK GREAT QUESTIONS

What if I told you you don't need to have a solution for every single problem that comes your way in order to be a competent and mature leader? Well that's exactly what I'm about to propose. Hopefully it's as refreshing to you as it is to me. And the best part about it is that it can dramatically improve your leadership influence as well. The alternative to responding with advice? Asking great questions.

Why Ask Questions?

Many leaders hesitate to ask questions because they fear it will make them appear weak. Leaders are supposed to have the all the answers, right? Unfortunately (or fortunately, depending on how you look at it), the world we live in has become so complex that it's simply not possible for *anyone* to have all the answers, no matter how tenured he or she is. But there are all kinds of benefits to asking questions, regardless of how much you know. Here are a few:

Great questions lead to great discoveries. Author and consultant Bobb Biehl likes to say, "If you ask profound questions, you get profound answers. If you ask shallow questions, you get shallow answers. If you ask no questions, you get no answers at all."

Great questions are the antidote to advice. Our own advice can be intelligent and fitting sometimes, but lousy or misinformed other times. Giving advice is easy and costs little, at least on the surface. In organizational settings however, a leader's advice can quickly get translated into a "direct order" with no room for further discussion.

Great questions develop the critical thinking skills of others. If you're a leader, the critical thinking skills of your team will likely determine how far you go. When you give answers, you get followers. When you give questions (and coach through the process of determining the best answer), you develop leaders.

Great questions delegate responsibility. At the end of the day, if you're the person everyone comes to with every problem, your leadership bar will remain low. Leaders need followers who can solve problems on their own. And keep in mind that a person is always more motivated to act on and own a solution he's come up with himself than to follow the guidance of someone else.

A person is always more motivated to act on and own a solution he's come up with himself than to follow the guidance of someone else.

What do Great Questions Look Like?

It's true that most leaders don't become great at asking questions until they become great at listening (something that should cause each of us to pause and consider). There's a learning process for everything. But in the meantime, let's consider some examples of what great, powerful questions look like.

Leading vs. Non-Leading Questions: A leading question proposes a solution in the form of a question. A non-leading question opens up the possibility for multiple solutions. Consider the differences between these two examples.

Leading: "What would happen if you tried having training meetings on Tuesdays?"

Non-Leading: "What are some different options for conducting training?"

Closed vs. Open-ended Questions: Closed questions require a "yes" or "no" answer while open-ended questions can have many outcomes.

Closed: "Have you thought about creating a new task force?"

Open-ended: "What are some ways you could approach this challenge?"

Advice vs. Possibility Questions: An advice question is basically just implied advice in the form of a question while possibility questions access the other person's insight.
Advice: "Couldn't you address that situation with the sales rep directly?"
Possibility: "How could you address that situation?"

Why vs. "Tell Me More" Questions: Why questions can feel abrasive and accusatory, regardless of intent. No one likes being interrogated. Using a "tell me more" approach opens up the dialogue.
Why: "Why did you decide to ship only seven orders?"
Tell me more: "Can you tell me more about the thought process for this shipment?"

Learning to ask great questions instead of giving advice is probably one of the hardest disciplines leaders encounter. (It's right up there with active listening!) I know by personal experience and from conducting training with seasoned leaders. The first step is to stop yourself from giving unsolicited advice. The next step is to respond with a question. The final step is to make that question a powerful one. My encouragement is to give it a try and stick with it. Ask someone to give you feedback on your question-asking ability. It'll be slow at first, but eventually start becoming natural. And the leaders you serve will develop right along with you.

Questions for Reflection

- Which of the negative types of questions do you tend to find yourself using the most?
- Which types of powerful questions do you think can make the biggest impact in your leadership interactions?
- In what situations can you begin to respond with a question rather than advice?

WHAT COACHING LEADERS DO DIFFERENTLY

"Coaching" has been a trending corporate buzzword in organizational leadership for well over a decade now. We're all familiar with athletics coaches. But when someone asks us to coach someone to learn a new skill or solve a problem, it's usually in a professional work context. What do coaches actually do — or do differently?

The interesting thing about coaching is how dynamic of a leadership role it is. Supervisors can coach. Mentors can coach. Peers can coach. Executive coaches can coach (obviously). Just about anyone can coach at one time or another.

Whether you have the opportunity to be coached or to be a coach, let's take a look at six things coaching leaders do that set them apart.

Coaches Don't Set the Agenda

Leaders must be proactive, which means taking responsibility to set the agenda in leadership situations. But coaching leaders are most concerned with the developmental process of the leader he or she is supporting. That means allowing the other person to take responsibility for determining the desired outcomes — and then working together to create a strategy to reach them.

Coaches Focus on the Future

Counselors often focus on understanding or interpreting the past. Coaches, on the other hand, focus on helping create the future. The past is over and done with — it can't change. Coaching leaders don't get sidetracked wading through past experiences of others. They help them focus on the goals they want to achieve.

Coaches Listen

Listening is hard work. If you don't think so, practice active listening the next time someone walks into your office. In most conversations, we either don't pay attention, listen with preconceived biases or simultaneously try to come up with solutions while the other person is talking. Coaching leaders have mastered the art of listening for the sake of understanding and maximizing the quality of the dialogue.

Coaches Ask Questions

Questions are the anecdote to unsolicited (or in some case, solicited) advice. It's not that advice is bad, it's just that advice often short-circuits the development process in others. Following someone else's advice is a lot easier than exercising critical thinking. It's also easier to avoid taking responsibility if the advice doesn't work. Even when they have great advice, coaching leaders start by asking powerful, open-ended questions to give the other person the chance to come up with their own best solution.

Coaches are Action-Oriented

Nice conversations are nice, but ultimately fruitless. Action-oriented conversations drive change. Coaching leaders demonstrate value to others by helping them translate ideas into action items. They help them weigh multiple options until they arrive at a decision. Another way is by helping to craft SMART goals and clarify next steps.[6]

Coaches Give Responsibility

Taking responsibility is Leadership 101. Giving responsibility is Leadership 102. Think about the difference. When we take responsibility, we develop ourselves. When we help someone else take responsibility, we develop them.[7] It's often easier to take responsibility for outcomes by providing quick direction and then moving on to the next thing. Giving responsibility — and supporting the other person along the way — takes more time and effort, but that's where true leadership growth happens.

Taking responsibility is Leadership 101. Giving responsibility is Leadership 102.

If you want to help others succeed, you've chosen a noble pursuit. But that's not enough. You've got to work at it — and it's hard work! But the reward is always worth it — especially when you find that the leaders you've coached start coaching others.

Questions for Reflection

- How have you coached others in the past? What were the results?
- How might you adjust your coaching approach for greater effectiveness?
- Who could benefit most from your intentional coaching?
- What opportunities for impromptu "coaching moments" might you have in any given day?

THE APPLAUSE OF A SINGLE HUMAN BEING

How can I add more zest to these program communications?

That was the question on my mind for a past corporate leadership program I managed. There had to be a better way to communicate with the leaders participating than simply nagging them to complete their assignments.

So in the next program email, I included an insightful reflection from "Kevin," since he was one of the several thousand leaders participating.

I didn't have to wait long for a response, but I was surprised by who it came from. Within minutes an email reply appeared from the company president. He had cc'd me in a reply directly to Kevin and included Kevin's entire executive chain of command. The president began by thanking him for his engagement in the program and leadership in his function and ended with a "proud to have you on the team!"

I didn't know anyone busier than the company president, but he still found time to give a personal kudos. I didn't know Kevin personally, but I bet he went home walking on air with a story to share with his family over dinner. *That was really fun to be a part of,* I thought. *I want to do this again.*

One of my favorite quotes of all-time comes from the 18th century English writer Samuel Johnson, who observed, "The applause of a single human being is of great consequence."

Each of us are "single human beings." We qualify. Your applause is of great consequence, and so is mine.

Celebrating the success of others is definitely a "nice" thing to do, but if we think a little deeper, it has some real benefits for us as well.

"The applause of a single human being is of great consequence."

— Samuel Johnson

Engage Them and Retain Them

According to a recent Gallup report, only one in three American workers said they received recognition or praise from their boss within the last week.[8] Not only that, under-recognized employees are twice as likely to actively seek outside employment.[9] It's no wonder Dale Carnegie was so emphatic about "giving honest, sincere appreciation."[10] It's much harder for employees to leave a boss who heaps appreciation their way.

Become More Aware of Others' Contributions

You've heard the old adage that "what you see is what you get." Need proof? Do you remember your last vehicle purchase? Suddenly it seemed half the other drivers on the road had the same car as you. You spotted the vehicle everywhere. Of course the number of cars didn't change — your awareness did. Become a "good-finder" and you may be surprised how much there is to notice.

Win Hearts... and Minds

How do you determine whether you trust someone? Is it because of logic or because of emotion? So often, we try to convince our followers and colleagues of the rationale for following our ideas when an emotional appeal would do a better job. When you win someone's heart, they will often give you their mind as well. The opposite is not always the case.

Showing honest and sincere appreciation is a sure fire way to appeal to the heart. Do this, and it will be much easier to sell your ideas as well.

Change the Culture

Have you ever been part of a "gotcha" culture? Unfortunately some people find fault like there is a reward for it. What if the "gotcha" was for doing something right instead of wrong?

In *Whale Done!* Ken Blanchard observed that SeaWorld trainers have learned the best way to turn a performance animal into a star is through constant and positive, rather than negative, reinforcement.[11] It's the same with people. Not only that, when enough leaders jump on board, the entire culture can shift.

It's a Ton of Fun!

When the president's email reply came through, I'll admit I didn't even read it right away. As soon as I realized what it was, I had to find a colleague to share it with. Even though I was an observer, it was the highlight of my day. We all have the ability to make someone else's day — and by extension, our own. Words and gestures matter. Even if you're known for being gruff, the invitation is open. You'll be the one who benefits most.

So what does applause have to do with leadership expertise? That's easy. People want to be influenced by leaders who value them. You may never be the foremost authority on leadership – that's the reality for almost everyone. But leadership influence starts with a genuine human commitment. Being generous with your applause will turn you into a trusted advisor other people seek.

Questions for Reflection

- Whose applause has been of great consequence to you?
- How would you rate the culture where you work? Is it an applause culture or a "gotcha" culture?
- Who deserves your applause?
- Who may not deserve your applause but would benefit from it nonetheless?

CONCLUSION

I'll never forget a conversation I had with my friend Laura. It must have taken place six or seven years ago. Laura was a young teacher with aspirations to become a principal one day. But she was really feeling the heat. On top of the daily pressure of managing a fifth grade classroom, she was responsible for organizing projects for the other more experienced teachers as part of her career track development. Some were supportive and others weren't — and let her know it. As the stress started to mount, it became clear: something had to change, either in the circumstances or inside of her.

In that moment, I realized I wanted to be Laura's leadership expert. I didn't know anything about teaching fifth grade or being a principal, but that's not what she needed. Laura also didn't need to know everything there is to know about leadership. She simply needed the next idea in actionable form that could keep her going. I knew I could help, if I made the effort to be available. That's usually the most important thing leadership experts can do: simply be available.

I've realized since then that most everyday leaders are like Laura. They've experienced some level of success, but they're stuck between the way things are now and the next level, whatever that represents. Something has to give. Having access to a trusted advisor nearby can make all the difference.

By now, I hope you realize that being a leadership expert is well within your reach. It's not a designation reserved only for a select few. You can join the club! The invitation has been made. Will you accept?

SPECIAL BONUS:

NINE WAYS TO BE THE BOSS EVERYONE WANTS TO WORK FOR

I hope this book has ignited a desire to develop your leadership to the next level. In this book, I've shared many ways you can build your leadership expertise right here, right now – independent from a formal leadership role. But what if you *are* responsible for leading a team? What can you do not only to hold down the fort but to become the leader others line up to follow?

In the opening pages I promised I would save a special bonus for everyone who made it to the end. Here it is: a free white paper *Nine Ways to Be the Boss Everyone Wants to Work For*. Download your copy today at http://www.nathanmagnuson.com/best-boss.

Also, if you found the information in this book useful, would you please do me two favors? First, will you leave an honest review on Amazon.com? And second, will you share it with a friend you believe has the potential for greater leadership impact?

ACKNOWLEDGMENTS

This book would probably still just be an idea or a draft sitting in a computer folder except for the help of many key people. I'd like to give credit and appreciation where it's due, starting here.

John W. Nichols – Thank you for turning these words into a well-designed book. Without your help, expertise and project management, this wouldn't have been possible!

Mark Miller & Bob Tiede – Thank you for the awesome endorsements. They give me something to continue to aspire to!

John Maloney – Thank you for your enthusiasm for nearly everything I've written, including the first draft of this book from 2014.

Nichole Vaux – Thank you for your design input.

Abigail Linhardt — Thank you so much for your last minute late night copy editing.

Chris Hendrix – Thank you for being my writing buddy (and friend!) since we met at the writers conference in 2012.

Launch Team – Thank you to everyone who joined my launch team and helped share this book's message.

NOTES

1. Truett Cathy, *It's Easier to Succeed Than to Fail* (Thomas Nelson, Inc., 1989). For more about Truett Cathy, visit: http://www.nathanmagnuson.com/leadership-profile-truett-cathy.

2. Zig Ziglar, *Born to Win* (Made for Success Publishing, 2017). For more about Zig Ziglar, visit: http://www.nathanmagnuson.com/leadership-profile-zig-ziglar.

3. Stephen R. Covey, *The 7 Habits of Highly Effective People* (Mango, 2017). For more about Stephen R. Covey, visit: http://www.nathanmagnuson.com/leadership-profile-stephen-covey.

4. Nathan Magnuson, "Leadership Profile: Jack Welch," *NathanMagnuson.com*, http://www.nathanmagnuson.com/leadership-profile-jack-welch.

5. Nathan Magnuson, "Reconciling Humility and Leadership," *NathanMagnuson.com*, http://www.nathanmagnuson.com/reconciling-humility-and-leadership.

6. Nathan Magnuson, "How SMART Are Your Goals?" *NathanMagnuson.com*, http://www.nathanmagnuson.com/how-smart-are-your-goals.

7. Nathan Magnuson, "What a Leadership Coach Won't Do For You," *NathanMagnuson.com*, http://www.nathanmagnuson.com/what-a-leadership-coach-wont-do-for-you.

8. Annamarie Mann & Nate Dvorak, "Employee Recognition: Low Cost, High Impact." Gallup, June 28, 2016, https://www.gallup.com/workplace/236441/employee-recognition-low-cost-high-impact.aspx.

9. Ibid.

10. Dale Carnegie, *How to Win Friends and Influence People* (Pocket Books, 1998). For more about Dale Carnegie, visit: http://www.nathanmagnuson.com/leadership-profile-dale-carnegie.

11. Ken Blanchard, Thad Lacinak, Chuck Tomkins & Jim Ballard, *Whale Done!* (Free Press, 2002).

ABOUT THE AUTHOR

Nathan Magnuson is a corporate leadership development consultant, coach and trainer. He's worked in a staff or consulting role with several Fortune 500 companies and large public service organizations, including Accenture, MASCO, FBI, and Defense Intelligence Agency. Nathan is also a military veteran, having served a tour with  the Army Special Operations in Operation Iraqi Freedom.

In addition to corporate work, Nathan is also an author and active author, with articles posted on his site NathanMagnuson.com and in various leadership publications.

Nathan grew up in Kansas City and resides in Dallas, TX. At any given time, you might find him enjoying downtown Dallas, watching football or collaborating with other leaders to bring the next big idea to life.

You can follow Nathan on Facebook, Twitter, LinkedIn or on his website.

www.facebook.com/NathanMagnusonLeadership

www.twitter.com/nathanmagnuson

www.linkedin.com/in/nathanmagnuson

www.nathanmagnuson.com

NATHAN'S RECOMMENDED READING

Leadership

- *How to Win Friends and Influence People* by Dale Carnegie
- *The 7 Habits of Highly Effective People* by Stephen R. Covey
- *Dare to Serve* by Cheryl Bachelder
- *Switch* by Chip Heath & Dan Heath
- *Good to Great* by Jim Collins
- *The Secret* by Ken Blanchard & Mark Miller
- *Extreme Ownership* by Jocko Willink & Leif Babin
- *The 21 Irrefutable Laws of Leadership* by John Maxwell
- *Start with Why* by Simon Sinek
- *Leading with the Heart* by Mike Krzyzewski & Donald Phillips

- *Leadership and Self-Deception* by The Arbinger Institute
- *Creativity, Inc.* by Ed Catmull
- *Great Leaders Grow* by Ken Blanchard & Mark Miller
- *The Five Dysfunctions of a Team* by Patrick Lencioni
- *Crucial Conversations* by Kerry Patterson, Joseph Grenny, Ron McMillan & Al Switzler
- *The 15 Invaluable Laws of Growth* by John Maxwell

Career

- *48 Days to the Work You Love* by Dan Miller
- *No More Dreaded Mondays* by Dan Miller
- *What Color is Your Parachute?* by Richard Bolles
- *Quitter* by Jon Acuff

Life

- *Rules of the Red Rubber Ball* by Kevin Carroll
- *Let Your Life Speak* by Parker Palmer
- *Decisive* by Chip Heath & Dan Heath
- *How to Stop Worrying and Start Living* by Dale Carnegie
- *Start* by Jon Acuff

29143569R00045

Made in the USA
Columbia, SC
21 October 2018